Crackle at Midnight

Poems

OTHER HEINEMANN FRONTLINERS

Upper Level

Cyprian Ekwensi:	*For a Roll of Parchment*
Patrick Fagbola:	*Kaduna Mafia*
Niyi Osundare:	*The Eye of the Earth (Poems)* **(Joint-Winner of the 1986 Commonwealth Poetry Prize)**
Rose Njoku:	*Withstand the Storm*
Jeremiah Essien:	*In the Shadow of Death*
Okinba Launko:	*Minted Coins (poems) (Winner of the Africa Zone of 1988 Dillions Commonwealth Poetry Prize)*
Chinua Achebe:	*Anthills of the Savannah*
Tess Onwueme:	*The Reign of Wazobia and other plays* Atabo
Oko:	*The Secret of the Sheik*
Tess Onwueme:	*Legacies (a play)*
Niyi Osundare:	*Songs of the Season (poems)*
Niyi Osundare:	*Midlife*
Niyi Osundare:	*Horses of Memory (poems)*
Afolabi A Adio-Moses:	*Flashes of Ideas and Reflections (poems)*
Tolu Ajayi:	*The Ghost of a Millionaire*
Oladele Akadiri:	*A Sin in the Convent*
Bridget Nwankwo:	*Drums of Destiny*
Iyorwuese H. Hagher:	*Mulkin Mata (a play)*
Sola Osofisan:	*Darksongs (poems) (Winner 1990 ANA Poetry Prize)*
Sola Osofisan:	*The Living and the Dead (Winner 1990 ANA Prose Prize)*
Femi Osofisan:	*Once Upon Four Robbers (a play)*
Femi Osofisan:	*Yungba Yungba and the Dance Contest*

Crackle at Midnight
Poems

Lupenga Mphande

 Heinemann Educational Books (Nigeria) Plc

HEINEMANN EDUCATIONAL BOOKS (NIGERIA) PLC
Head Office: 1 Ighodaro Road, Jericho, P.M.B. 5205, Ibadan
Phone: (02) 2412268, 2410943; *Telex:* 31113 HEBOOKS NG
Fax: (02) 2411089, 2413237; *Cable:* HEBOOK, Ibadan.

Area Offices and Branches
Abeokuta. Akure. Bauchi. Benin City. Calabar. Enugu. Ibadan
Ikeja. Ilorin. Jos. Kano. Katsina. Maiduguri. Makurdi. Minna
Owerri. Port Harcourt. Sokoto. Uyo. Yola. Zaria

© Lupenga Mphande 1998
First Published 1998

ISBN 978 129 347 0

All Rights Reserved

No part of this publication may be reproduced, stored in a retrieval system or transmitted in any form or by any means, electronic, mechanical, photocopying, recording, or otherwise, without the prior permission of Heinemann Educational Books (Nigeria) Plc.

This book is sold subject to the condition that it should not by way of trade or otherwise be lent, re-sold, hired out or otherwise circulated without the publisher's prior consent in any form of binding or cover other than that in which it is published and without a similar condition including this condition being imposed on the subsequent purchaser.

Printed and bound in Nigeria by
Cargo Press, Lagos.

Statement

Lupenga Mphande's poetry is concerned with rural dwellers and how they relate to their environment. In his own way, Mphande uses nature to defend African traditions in a most fascinating way. In many of his poems there is no distance between the poet and the life he describes, using a narrative style that is steady and sure, and employing an exile motif which represents something truly original in his work. Mphande has a knack for "showing" rather than telling what he means, using his power of description to full effect with vivid, sensuous imagery that transports the reader to feel, see, and hear what the poet creates, sometimes achieving, like in In "Search for a bride," a startling juxtaposition.

Frank Chipasula has said that Lupenga Mphande's poetry "flourishes on irony, understatement, euphemism, and indirection, and marries wit to a prophetic and apocalyptic vision," and that his "style is contemplative and strongly descriptive, yielding carefully ordered, long, fluid lines, which pulsate with the rhythm of nature. He has a keen eye and a sharp ear, and his poems teem with sensuous images of cicadas, mosquitoes, hills, ridges, valleys, trees, grasslands, streams, and brooks. His experiments with full rhyme and half and near rhyme often produce the effect of spontaneous movement and sound in rural landscapes, which he loves to paint in words. Of all the Malawian poets, he is perhaps the only one who has faithfully, and lovingly rendered the beauty of rural Malawi, exemplifying the intimacy many of us feel with the land. In some poems, he juxtaposes the beauty of the land with the violence perpetuated on innocent peasants by their insensitive masters, producing a shocking effect. '(When My Brothers Come Home: Poems from Central and South Africa.)'

Lupenga Mphande was born at Thoza, northern Malawi. He did his primary school education at Embangweni Presbyterian Mission School, and has a B.A. degree from the University of Malawi, an M.A. in Linguistics from the University of Lancaster, and a Ph.D. in Linguistics from the University of Texas at Austin. He taught at the University of Malawi before going into exile, and is at present teaching at Ohio State University in the United States of America. Mphande's poems and critical works have been widely published in literary journals, poetry magazines, anthologies and books, and he has won several literary awards including the 'BBC Arts and African Poetry Award' in England.

Contents .... *Page*

Statement vii

I 1

Princess of the Plateau

II 4

On the Vipya

III 6

Keep Young When Winter Comes

IV 8

Shooting the Guineafowl *(for Anthony Nazombe)*

V 11

Bush Gambols

VI 14

The Lone Tree of Thoza

VII 17

An Outing on Dedza Mountain

VIII 19

Cutting the Millet Stalks

IX 20

Along the Rift Valley

X 23

Thoza View

XI 26

Bushfires

XII 28

A Tiny Lifespan

XIII 30

Snapping an Old Tree

XIV 32

A Crackle at Midnight

XV 34

Winter Morning

XVI 36

What I like Best

XVII	38
Where I was Born	
XVIII	42
The Fig Tree	
XIX	45
A Dance in the Kraal	
XX	48
Scanning for Rain	
XXI	51
The Refugees	
XXII	53
The Procession	
XXIII	55
Visiting Friends	
XXIV	58
Returning to Thoza	
XXV	61

My Grandfather

XXVI 63

Shrine Revisited

XXVII 66

How Shall I Know?

XXVIII 69

Touch of a Cure

XXIX 71

Beyond the Horizon

XXX 73

The School Bully

XXXI 76

Life of a Rich Man

XXXII 78

Village Headman Jenjewe

XXXIII 81

Where to Find Me

XXXIV 84

Easter at Embangweni

XXXV 86

Palsied Tyrant *(for Jack Mapanje)*

XXXVI 88

They took Suzgo away

XXXVII 90

Marginals

XXXVIII 92

Getting Past the Darkside *(for Orton Ching'oli Chirwa)*

XXXIX 95

The Noose

XL 97

Charred Pegs *(for Vera Chirwa)*

XLI 99

Austin, Frank and I

XLII 102

Freeing the Barbarians

XLIII 104

Charged with Treason *(for the mother of Amnon Phiri)*

XLIV	107
War Birds	
XLV	109
Dance of a Guerilla	
XLVI	111
I was Sent For	
XLVII	113
The Anvil	
XLVIII	116
We Shall be at the End	
XLIX	118
Ululations to a New Moon	
L	120
Strolling Down the Shoreline	
LI	122
Didn't We?	
LII	125
Courting Tasiyana	

LIII	127
Paying Lobola	
LIV	130
Maria's Photograph	
LV	132
Perdita	
LVI	135
A Letter to Anjana	
LVII	139
Strange Ways	
LVIII	142
Do You Remember?	
LIX	144
The Feet of a Dancer *(for Natasha, watching her play the viola)*	
LX	146
Search For a Bride	

I
Princess of the Plateau

I, even I, who gallop with zebras in the wind at dawn
Saw lady of the plateau rise at cock's crow silhouetted against
Cloud shades of grey in dry tinted air and merge with lake's
Sun flames as she strode over morning haze to interview virgins

I, even I, know the paths through the plateau
Whose breeze I breathe;

She sauntered along pebbles in shimmers of her bead necklace,
Sepia brown her turban, mountain dun her fan, fire amber
Her sandals, her shawl black, red, green undulating free
In the breeze to the flutter of palmleaves along the shore

I, even I, know the paths through the plateau
Whose breeze I breathe;

She raced against otters in streams, shielding the fish
Sprinted past packs of wolves, tooting her horn at the antelope
Of mottled mtowa her bow, arrows shine silver-shafts flickering
In sun's rays as she darted between hoofmarks tracking poachers

I, even I, know the paths through the plateau
Whose breathe I breathe;

The princess sang to the wind in the yellow and blue sunset,
Pausing among poolside poinsettias, edged by fragrant reeds
Stooping in flower, ivory white her teeth, sparkling stars her eyes
Her voice crystallizing into rain as she knelt in supplication

I, even I, know the paths through the plateau
Whose breathe I breathe.

II
On the Vipya

I sit in a sea of pink grass high up the Vipya plateau,
All around wild flowers sparkle like stars against
A lake breeze that blows the grass to endless waves,
All quiet save sounds of hill birds in the distance
As I watch two blue cranes pirouette a love dance
Fascinated by procreate nature in a trance;

The soft black earth staggers into water springs,
Waterplants grow in still pools which overflow into
Rivulets of thin silver cords-- this shinning water,
This land of absolute fragrance and restless green
Where veils fall with thunder and roam gorges
And hills fold and fold again;

I like to watch rains come to the plateau in December,
Rivulets stream into brown waves that tow away
Gigantic boulders and puny works of man
Or cattle egrets whiten banks of the Dwambazi--
The only sign that the lake is near, that ultimate beauty,
The flaming waters, shimmers of unforgettable memories;

But the Vipya and its rivulets, waterfalls and lake
Has its tale: there is a groyne of stones piled up on
A riverside anthill past the creek where fishermen stand
With long rods silhouetted against a flawless sky.
They say in broad daylight a woman was brangeoned to death there
By a jilted lover. She roams the banks on crescent moon-nights
When the pool is clear, water deep and grass emerald green.

III
Keep Young When Winter Comes

I hastened from the still dark city, shivering,
Anxious to get out of looming shadows of tall buildings.
In the country I padded silently, glowing
In the new light of the sun brightening over the ridge;

Through whips of mist rising in the still air
I lingered under a fig tree, sun's rays filtering through
Boughs, dripping soundlessly on dry leaves. Long-tailed
Mouse birds hid their fluffy heads in bunches of figs;

Across the haze where leaves had fallen
I could hear the clear still call of a dove:
Why so sad (if sad he is) when bright sun

Lightens above the ridge and touches the fluff.
Winter gale, perhaps, unveils his feathery blanket
And peeps bare at his skin, sooty-grey
Like an old woman's hair.

I saw another dove echo-sounding noon, looping
From twig to twig, cooing an urgency to all:
Come to the wilds, keep young when winter comes
Come to the wilds, keep young when winter comes.

IV
Shooting the Guineafowl
(for Anthony Nazombe)

Just as the sun had reached its limits, I paused
By a fig tree to contemplate quitting.
Just then, a guineafowl stuttered in the valley air,
Sooty-black, all spotted with white, and
He examined his perch on the euphorbia in the sunlight.
I had hunted him everywhere the whole day.
Now I was pleased to have found him, so
I plucked taut the sinew of my mutowa bow
And aimed my sharp-ended arrow, thinking:
"Under the arch of the blue sky,
Across the clear plain of the veld
The shaft will flicker in the setting sun,
The blade whiz through the air.
I will shoot it straight -
Straight to the heart!
But I will not kill him where he perches,
Glazed against the orange sunset like a spirit."

"Will he break upstream, against the wind, towards the conical hill
With nape exposed, violet-blue, in the dissolving light –
Casque bobbing, wattles flapping side to side?
Will he glide heavily down the valley, towards the overgrowth,
Taunting noisily as he drops, kek.. kek.. kek,
With wings spread, with tail fanned?
Or will he aim for the open space behind the eucalyptus
And crashland into undergrowth, racing on swift legs

To hide in the low bush of aloes?"
No! the guineafowl shot into air like
An arrow turning back on a bowman.
Tell me, how am I to shoot a keening bird
When he's perched upon my bow?

V
Bush Gambols

I was hunter of the veld,
in season I set fires to clear bush
and let ash nurture new pasture.
From dawn till sundown, each day,
I roamed charred thickets,
set traps in tracks by waterholes,
and trudged home, a reedbuck or guineafowl
lashed over my shoulder.
But there was one game forbidden
to all: white-tailed hare
that burrows in old graves
and shares ancestry with our spirits.

It is foolish to look in the sun
with naked eyes, or invite night
in daytime. Only blinded fools
look at the nakedness of an old man.

When I set out to inspect traps by
the creek I had a strange feeling
of something in the air, but something
led me on. Grass moved, I thought,
and the trap twanged bent - it was
a hare struggling to free itself.
I lunged with my knobkerrie,
putting an end to its life.

At midday I sat by the riverbank,
made fire by friction.
I flayed the animal on green leaves,

laid its skin by the fire
and set out to fetch more wood.
When I returned something moved
in the grass, something with long ears,
wagging its scut, spurting blood
in its wake. Something was wrong, I knew,
when a skinless hot-blooded animal
has to wriggle in terror across the hot sun.
Too late, I remembered, the warning not to harm the white-tailed hare
that burrows by the creek,
and I wept in sorrow.

I must return his coat, I thought,
lest the tropical sun scorch his back.
I range the charred veld now
in season and out, looking for the white-tailed hare.
I want to befriend him, patter about
summer herbs and name him after my son.

VI
The Lone Tree of Thoza

The tree has stood there all alone for ages, they say,
Stark as seemingly dead as rubbles of grey boulders,
The only tree above the conical rocks of the village hill;

Hunters and herdsboys swore they could hear clearly
Riding on mountain winds and the twitter of birds

Its age old lament. But one sunny afternoon in the wet of
First rains a flash of winged insects hovered over dry twigs,
Swirled in harmony to the hues of the rainbow,

And the lone tree of Thoza put out leaves and bright flowers
which brought bees and humming birds, and, like a zither player,

Sent out waves of sweet melodies that reverberated
from hills, gorges, creeks, ripples and marshes beyond
Until winds and twittering birds were hushed and still;

What could it be, asked hunters and herdsboys alike,
That brought the Thoza tree back from the mountain dead?

What magic bee or nectar god sheltered there seeded dry
Boughs and twigs with lustre of lyrical charm and fragrance
Which only yesterday stood cracked and stark like a stele?

But village elders said they did not know, for none
Could see what lay inside the tree cavities and hillcaves;

'Only a trickle of honey in the season,' was all I got
When I dared inquire from those old and young who had
Seen the tree blossom. Bees came buzzing, birds went

Humming, while the lone tree of Thoza swayed in the wind
Bidding villages join to sing and rejoice in its new foliage.

VII
An Outing on Dedza Mountain

I strolled the ancient slopes of dedza
past the radio mast
glowing red in the sun's rays
and paused briefly fro breath.
I sat still in dew
amid grey boulders
shadowing young pine
and thought about the rocks.
I marvelled at the proximity
of heaven and earth at sunrise
seen from these primordial ranges
that trail to the lake.
From far away
over green tropical bushes
I heard geology students
whistling to twitters of birds.
I watched dewdrops dissipate
from pine leaves in lambent fog.
The student on an outing, I
was sure, will obliterate
my solitary footprints
with their own.

VIII
Cutting the Millet Stalks

We have always done it at home
Cutting the millet stalks in the odour
Of ripening grass in June, before birds
In various plumage and call zoom
To take the field in a flutter,
Grain-feasting, making a great noise.
We have always done it in the village
Invading the field from all sides
With knives and whetstones slung
By shoulders, and in a swoop we squat
Hopping like frogs in season, warbling
In chorus, reaping the field bare.

IX
Along the Rift Valley

A few years ago I walked
along the rift valley and watched
villagers rise with dawn, plough
behind teams of oxen, singing,
bracing against morning mist,
making maize fields lush and broody
after the rains. Now tobacco farmers
mount tractors at noon, rip
the soil sour, and thrive.
Puffs of smoke blight through
valley air and drown for ever
love songs of thrushes.

X
Thoza View

I like the view of Thoza from ridges below
    laced with springs,
Patchwork fields lush and green,
    staggered with mlombwa trees
And boulders pocked with grey
    that trail hills to the lake.
I like walking spacious woods
    on edges peopled with sunbirds,
Rambling criss-cross waves of fields
    that dot the landscape.
In season bee hunters swarm the hills,
    yodel to honey-guides
Rain-washed hills rise shrouded in green canopies
    and wafts of lilac fragrance
Permeate village dwellings along greenbanks
    with reeds flowering in white --
Only in Thoza, and only here can you bask
    in so much sunshine

But closer up, way beyond dotted dwellings
Where the cool hillsun gives way
To a cold glittering night sky
I hear people ride hyenas in the dark:
I have walked along past Ng'onomo's kraal
Right up to Hora where Ngoni conquerors
Were warped in their sleep by their slaves.
At Ephangweni I see a hundred years later
How the chief there inverts his court;

Girls in his area are loose
And powerful men age early.
Among themselves, the people say
One cannot see Thoza through the haze.

XI
Bushfires

For nearly a month since lightning
struck and set a tree ablaze
a forest fire devoured the bluff
of Malosa hill. It flamed night and
day whichever way the mountain
winds blew. One day it raged and
roared across hundreds and hundreds
of acres towards Machinga, and
on others it smouldered down villages;

Yesterday the bushfire reached us. It burned down Mkuli
church and charred
the school pine plantation. I hear
bushfires are good for forest: they clear
the undergrowth for new sprouts,
provide pasture for grazing, and assist
the hunter with game. But surely
old trees wail in summer blazes
to the chagrin of the sun and thunder.

XII
A Tiny Lifespan

First bee comes and zipps
a funny sound across morning drone,
warmed by sun and hope of honey,
always she works, she knows nothing
else. A bee-eater swoops, glides, catapults,
scrabbles, and snaps her tiny lifespan. Ninety
die before the first gets back to the hive.

XIII
Snapping of an Old Tree

Patriach of the village woodland, the muwula
Tree had stood there for ages, they said,
A playground to children, a counterpose
To capricious nature. In summer elders sat
Under its shade, hiding from broiling noon,
And in drought children still bounced in
The branches and ate its fruit. But one day
The tree was heard to groan in the wind
And its bark cracked from a woodlouse bite
That turned the fruits sour. Sapplings,
Sceptics among undergrowths, did not know
The cure and did not throw a sop to the pain.
A whirlwind came that holwed throughout
The murky night, pulling at the tree, and
The muwula bent crazily in the wind,
Until at dawn a buttress root
Weakened and the tree snapped at the base,
Crashing into the undergrowth with a
Thunderous wail that shook the village.

XIV
A Crackle at Midnight

Kids' moon-games noise faded into slumber, and drowsy
Villagers retired, reflecting on the day's work, wishing
For better luck in future. As they said farewells
To each other and groped for sleeping mats a slow intrusion
Appeared on the horizon, a red balloon flikering like a halo;

Insipidly, in the quiet of the night a breeze fanned the fire
Into rustling flames that rolled down the plateau and crashed
Through village firebreaks. People scrambled from their houses
Grasping children, shaken and awed as the element engulfed
Grass thatch in a lurid glow;

They tore down tree branches and banana leaves to thrash out
The inferno and laboured half naked, radiant in sweat, dazed
By the incarnation of gods wrath. Others ran to the byre
To save animals and soon there was a stampede as cattle
And goats bolted at the smell of fire, mooing, bleating,

Knocking down everything in their way. In seconds
The conflagration swept past and was gone. Occasionally
Roofs collapsed, releasing brilliance and beauty when shooting
Sparks lit up the night and the village resounded with wails
Of relatives searching for casualties in the debris.

XV
Winter Morning

Not all is drab on a winter morning;
Colours come, not flamboyant as in summer
But hidden like flavours in the sky--
More subtle and fragrant.
Only a hill away beyond the church
Earth is no longer olive green pock marks
Where gathered leaves defy winter chill.

XVI
What I like Best

What I like best is the view of a village
From atop an opposing ridge
To watch a farmer work his field,
Till the land for better yield
Youths carting produce across a gully
Yodel to the sun in the valley,
Women sing in chorus around the byre,
Tell stories around a fire.
Villagers pause, having finished a task,
Watch each little star wake at dusk.
I like chirps of birds and crickets at dawn,
Humming of bees when petals are drawn.

But when the village is in drought
Listen to wailing farmers
Their crops wilting in broiling heat
The lament of mothers at dry wells
Their children whimpering on their backs
Groan of men in moonlight hearing
Hisses of wind through cracks in the wall,
Listen to the coughs at midnight
The silence that follows a groan,
Listen, and then tell me what you like best.

XVII
Where I was Born

"The names that touched our childish play." Yeats, 1913

Follow cow tracks skirting lush fields dotting the countryside
And ascend a staggered range of hills. You'll see towering
Families of cumulus spread like birds over brooks to crest
Into brilliant white against the blue.
If you come to Thoza peak and see green hills
That merge with clouds, listen to songs of leaves
In the wind, look for wispy edges of hail crystals
In raindrops and think of me, dear friend, in the place
I was born. I was the herdsboy who roamed the velds,
But, exiled now, wanders lonely with the cloud.

Up the hill there is a chill in the air.
A bracing wind veers into a violent updraft
And clouds push turrets up from the summit.
Condensation of ice crystals falls as rain. But When thunder-
clouds form into eddies and clear,
And the sun appears through bluish patches
And flushes out fluttering insects from sunny sides of boulders
Swirling around colours of the rainbow,
Know I was the youth who knew the paths criss-
Crossing the staggered hills evading colonial soldiers,
The scout who sighted the dwellings of informers
And guided the patriotic fighters at dawn.

Kamwana betrayed, Domingo rose to take his place

And descended on Jenda fighting to the end. Chikuse, Kufa
And others charged with fury past Chilembwe's staked head
But fell like dry leaves against the charging British battery.
At the Nkhata Bay quay men and women braved the breeze
And were mowed down in their blood--
All over the land, women with sickles encircled the invaders
To liberate their land and take back what was theirs.
I was the youth who knew the fighters by name,
The errand boy who survived by exploits of my own,
Who chronicled events and therefore remembers;

When I am gone, turned into dust like our heroes,
Think of me, do not let me die:
Think of me in cracked leaves of aloes
Think of me in the clock ticking above you
Think of me in courtroom monotones
Think of me in silence of the classroom
Think of our true heroes who lost their lives
So that we can fight for our own, think of me;

Come to Thoza, stay to walk through villages scattered on
Ridge slopes. Ask folks working in fields about the antelopes,
Herbs and chronicles that lace their lives. Ask them about
Mzikubola, Kaswaya, Tasiyana, Sambizga, Peru-pezu, Wema,
And others; or let them tell you about kalulu, bongololo
And more -- stories I so much loved in youth.
And one of them might even tell - albeit in whispers -
About the tyrant who at a swish of his flywhisk

Mowed people into dust, unaware that even dust
Will rise in the wind and soar to the sky.

XVIII
The Fig Tree

Looking up from my verandah, wide-eyed
In the starlight, I watch the sky frame
the fig tree, branches strung out
Like brooding hen, fragrant.
Blossom fills the night air, leaves
flash, rustling, swaying
above my thatch, and I step closer.
What is its age, I wonder;

In cold seasons when I sit by the fireside
I can hear the tree wail in the night,
its tracery seething in the breeze
as its old leaves lift into the air
and flutter down to the boulders below;

In the hot season the village council
holds its court in the tree shade,
and elders dispense weighty issues
while leaves listen and mousebirds
bicker with squirrels over ripe figs,
cobbling the lawn with their droppings.
The village ponders: how did the tree come to be?
The tree, they know, has stood there rooted
in the red soil, a delight to the eye,
a monument to whoever planted it;

And when the village was built
young people etched their names

in the tree bark for posterity.
But now, I hear, times being as they are,
the council has voted to cut the tree down
and barter the wood away to tobacco farmers.

XIX
A Dance in the Kraal

Sacrifices, our elders say, are no means to therapy,
Pain that is coiled will spring again. The ache
In my belly persists, blazing a trail to my grave.
How many times have I geared up in skins for ingoma,
Rising in the kraal quivering to chimes of anklebells
Only to watch intersections in my sisal skirt snap
At the seams at the apex of a dungthud? How many
Times have I warmed to drum rhythms, revved up
Tempo, cued for a new song only to stagger in mid-step
Lost, hearing foreign tunes mellowing over handclapping?

The moon has occluded a star, say our diviners,
And she will soon pass into the shadow of the earth
In another lunar eclipse, hiding bones of children
Mortalized in the Kalahari. How many times
Have I shuffled along the village path shouldering
Rolled reed mats? How many times have I choked on dust
While trying to keep count of mounds at the village yard?
Yet the government agent says our children's bellies extend
Because of kwashiorkor, but didn't I grow cucumbers,
Pumpkins, maize and millet before they brought
Healing herbicides that soured the healthy earth?
We are a strong breed, my kinsmen, a surviving race.
But tell me, how many in our clan were ferried away
In dhows through Zanzibar to grow cloves?
How many were shackled across the Atlantic, fettered
To droop in the sugar and cotton fields? How many
Were left in this village after warfts from gunpowder

Had settled, our youths driven to waist beads of whiskey?
But I tell you this: foreign craze will fade.
Our altars cleansed, crops replanted, drums set,
Our children will rise again to dance in the kraal.
There will be another!

XX
Scanning for Rain

We set out at dawn, travelling light against scorching
Heat waves, processing slowly toward the sacred
Rock, messengers to signal Leza of lightning and thunder
Who lives in the rainbow: 'Chiuta, creator of fire and rain,
Who makes mountains tremble and rivers flood
Listen to cries of children in the hot sun
Listen to bleating of goats and mooing of cows
Intercede on our behalf and bring us rain.' I was the youth
To fetch *kowela* the rainbird, a witness to the sacrifice;

We slit the bird by the riverbank, tied its entrails
To the casque and threw them into eddies: 'You Leza, who is
Spirit, hear our prayer. We praise you the same way
As our forefathers: *Tomoka, Sambizga, NyaChunda* praised you
Under this same rock, and you heard them
And brought them rain of prosperity. We beseech you
Enjoin the cycle, be on our side and end the drought.
Let the scarlet of the hornbill glow into life-giving rain,
Be with us always, we who are your children;'

We went round the sacred rock several times,
Sprinkling millet gruel around the base.
The fire was drilled and sacrifices made.
I was a witness at the riverside, one who stood
To point out the morning star and scan for rain clouds.
A patch appeared, wept alligator tears, then blew away.
After libation we filed home, silent, our eyes glazed over.

Trees stooped bare, the sky remained purple blue.
No other clouds formed;

An eerie silence enveloped the village, occasionally
Broken by stench and buzz of goldflies that sparkled
In bright sun, marking out bloating children. 'The earth
Cannot hold any more bodies,' wailed grave-diggers,
And the earth was hard. Acres and acres of farmland
Were left soured. Rain did not come.

XXI
The Refugees

Whether they journey across
the Kalahari, Ogaden, or Sahel,
whether they criss-cross the Nile,
Zambezi, or Congo tributaries,
they have but one purpose:
a flight from swerltering drought
        that wilts their crops, depletes their stock
a flight from ethnic rivalies
        that maim their children, kill their kins
a flight from cross-fire heat of ideologies
        that sizzle their minds, numbs their senses.
They cram baskets (lucky ones),
babies on their backs, and walk
in the hot sun, journeying
to seek refuge, in hope of food,
in hope of peace.

XXII
The Procession

We moved in a procession
towards a dug-up mound
at the village border,
only the initiated stepped in
as bearers, the rest shuffled
solemnly in the wings,
feet flattening the bush

> I remember
> The two of us herding
> Goats, chasing rabbits
> In surrounding anthills...
> Who will accompany me now?

".... The creator," said the minister
clasping wet earth, "the creator
made us of this clay, and to it
we return after our sojourn...
dust to dust. Amen."

As the crowd straggled home
I lingered by the shrubs
looking at the red mound,
half expecting him to rise
and follow me. All I heard
was the church bell "gong...gong...
gone..."

XXIII
Visiting Friends

I mean to visit Thoza one more time
Touch again the rock I haven't seen
Since banishment at the hands of that upstart.
While at Thoza I mean to visit Mtowole and Ephangweni
In January when the green brooks at sunrise
Are soaked in tints of gold that make a mockery of heaven
And the rainstorms, for weeks sometimes,
Dare you venture one step beyond your grass thatched verandah.
I want to once again take the herd out to pasture
Eat wild fruits while the cows graze
And, as in the past, I will sing again
Songs of the season in echo to thrushes,
And carve fighting bulls from clay
By the riverside at noon.

Some distance west of my village
Down the reedy valley of Lwasozi
Two of my childhood friends lie in the sand
Barely two miles from each other,
And there on a Sunday morning
I mean to go and visit
Friends I have not seen in decades.
Wet to the skin, perhaps,
I will brave the storm alone, if need be,
Wade across Lwasozi sand, step by step
Grasping at river reeds for support,
Slashing the grass with my feet, and
Look for their moulds on which to plant the flowers,

I will not be deterred, for the journey has to be made.
When a school boy at Embangweni
I never thought for a moment
That Tichafa and Vuso would so soon
Depart for those god forsaken sandbanks,
Leaving me alone to build the schools and clinics
Of our childhood dreams.

XXIV
Returning to Thoza

It was early morning when I dropped off
the bus at Thoza junction and watched mist lift from brooks.
It was a glorious morning
drenched in Spring sunlight, sun's rays
turning dewdrops into diamonds among flowers
of lilies and poinsettia After years of absence
browsing in concrete jungles abroad
I stood silenced by a presence in the air
emanating, I was sure, from solitary
outcrops of rocks scattered over ridges.
In the valley below the deciduous
were abloom, and I bathed in wafts
of blossoms of season, struck by promise
of happiness and joy.
Then I picked my way through familiar villages,
satiated with pleasurable feelings at the chatter
of women tending their fires, the clatter of ox carts
over river pebbles, the chirrup of children
shambling up to me.

We all have birthmarks and stand in awe of the stars,
it is not good for the old to linger out in the cold.
When I look back now at my age I see moments
of hope and despair, times I did not say what I should
have said, did not do what I ought to have done,
when, out of fear, I remained silent. Once,
I stretched my hand to pass a mango fruit, but a child
bit my finger and I withdrew my hand. I cut a rose

in the morning but its blossom wilted in the sun
enroute to the intended. I have been a man sitting
on the fence, listening to the wind at midnight,
fearing aches of a cold touch. I have written
many novels in titles only.

Yet my body attains a certain rebirth
on these ridges where I first toddled bare.
In days of tyranny and tribulation
I depend now on this feeling:
Thoza my village waits for me.

XXV
My Grandfather

He was always careful with his questions, and
Everytime my Grandfather stamped his stick
It left a circle on the weathered side of the village path.
A fault had left a crack in the wall
That drew moisture in, and in dry season
Left a stain over the dung-smeared wall.
Kneading wet clay, I thought of the many bull fights
I could watch if only I had thorns for horns
And breath enough to bellow for my herd.
When they came out his words hung in the dry air:
"Tell me," he said, "where did you leave your herd?"
I looked at my mother on the verandah, thinking:
She still thinks I am made of clay and that exposed
To a hailstorm I would melt into bits of earth.
A stinging ant crawled toward my Grandfather
But thought better and edged away from his stick.
"By the waterhole," I said. "Basking at the edge of the anthill.
They were not dry enough, so I left them in the sun,
And how splendid they looked!"
"No! no!" he said. "Why did you leave the goats
To be mauled by a pack of leopards?
How could you run away and abandon them?"
I recalled how earlier that day a leopard had snatched two goats.
"But I did not abandon them," I said. "I was there!" And
I wanted to shout "It wasn't my fault!" But
Tears filled my eyes, and sobs stole my speech.
All I could do was hold fast to Grandfather,

Head down, trying to catch back my breath.
"Child," mother called to me. "Leave your Grandfather be,"
And she pried my fingers from around Grandfather's stick.

XXVI
Shrine Revisited

When we revisited the riverside shrine
In the breezy tropical moonlight
We found the surrounding grass
Bent into a grey perpetual prayer
As if in old age turned religious;
Deciduous trees had their leaves falling
The fallen leaves attaining a lustre
That in death acquired a more beautiful tinge.

XXVII
How Shall I Know

In this age of super-colliders
where energy never flags,
in this age of plastic surgery
where beauty never fades,
in this age of space journeys
when a season becomes an entire lifetime
      how shall I know if my life
      is not just an echo?

Beauty, they say, shines because of ugliness,
loneliness follows company as darkness day.
It is space within that makes winnowing basket useful,
crack in the wall that lets in light and air.
But it is pettiness that clouds our vision,
      how shall I know if my life
      is not just refraction?

Young professionals, we are hollow men
separated from one another and exhausted.
We walk this earth in trendy suits,
holding attache cases, with no memories.
Competition nourishes our alienation, we resent
what we lack and are jealous of neighbours.
Impatience fosters resignation - for greed
we hoard, bask in city lights that block out
the moon and stars. Promises forgotten, integrity
compromised, our love is casual and we remain aloof.
      How shall I know if my life
      is not just a sputter in a void?

I have often walked round Thoza hill
trying to recollect my past. Every so often
I feel like talking to the crops of rocks
that surround the base, to introduce myself,
and tell the hill I am Tomoka's grandson just returned
from studies abroad. I want to explain
how a crazy silicon chip marred lift-off,
how I was flung so far into galaxy I cannot remember.
But each time I hesitate, fearing what the hill would say.

XXVIII
Touch of a Cure

His touch was once the cure
to scabies, polyps, migraine headaches
and other ailments that hospitals failed
to treat. Everything he touched was cured
of the blight or whatever people said they
suffered from at the time, and people flocked
to him like sheep to a well: some brought
Swiss watches, others fleets of Mercedes-Benzs
and those poor tethered goats at his door as gifts
in exchange for nirvana. And he took them all
to his harem while his followers bathed in rivers
he crossed, chewed barks and roots of trees
he touched, and everyone scrambled for his frail handshake.

"Come forth!" he would shout from the balcony
of his mansion in the hills, and those afflicted
or in anguish (and many were) thrashed
through bush to his hermitage. Even at night
they followed bats as their navigators through
the paths of the plateau. I hear he twitches
at the mouth now: the light has moved too far,
and he has suffered an eclipse --
he is no longer what he was.
He lives now alone in his huge mansion,
and when the moon rises full in the east
he paces the veranda and trains his ears to the wind.
They say he hears nothing, and no longer knows
the herb for the cure.

XXIX
Beyond the Horizon

Why do you gape
    at my stare?
You look but can't see
    for your images are boys
too simple in their form.

You frown at the grey beard
    I fondle?
But do you realise I'm still
    chasing a truth
You have yet to seek?

Do not laugh at the thinness
    of my ear:
I hear the sounds you miss
    silent but pertinent
in the moonlit winds

Reach out beyond the labyrinths
    of modernity
for roots forgotten

xxx
The School Bully

In village grounds
at home
we plucked out whetstones
pestles and mortars,
instrument for moongames
in the evening.
Not so at school;

During morning break
at school
we, children from surrounding
villages, played
on a patch of sand in the school yard,
whistled to mouse birds
in the kachere trees -
until Mugoba came!
He was big, he was mean,
and I didn't know what
must have annoyed him
but he picked on me.

He keeps on coming
his eyes red
and I back to a tree
thinking: this is it,
at a clap
a rhinocerous advances,
his tail taut.

Until he stumbles over a straw
then he charges!
Mugoba is a rhino
looking for a straw;

Where will I be
when he charges?
I asked myself.
Flat out on the grass
with a broken nose,
Mugoba piddling on me?
 Or miles from here
tearing bush, panting for breath?
Or should I brace up
and let what happens
happen?

I didn't know for certain
as I landed a straight left
as I let loose a straight left
as I aimed a straight left
as I jabbed with a right
as I landed a left uppercut...
and he staggered
once
doubled
slumped down to the floor

XXXI
Life of a Rich Man

He heard in his sleep shrills of his tenants:
"Howl, howl Kamuzunguzeni for the miseries
That are coming upon you.
You took our goats, our cows, our chicken.
Cast down Nimrod and his Babel tower!"
He opened the mullioned window and listened.
It was the year of the drought. The crescent
shone out, but there were no moon-games.
He thought he heard sobs of women below
covering groans of children. He retreated
to the inner mansion, barred doors,
and lay down with his gun.
Throughout the night he hallooed, chasing
thieves in his sleep, and woke at daybreak
all bleary-eyed and hoarse. He tiptoed
to the strongroom, counted his gold, drooping.

XXXII
Village Headman Jenjewe

Truly exotic! Cattle herders, creatures from the wild they
        call us
        and aim their cameras at our pierced ear lobes.
No aeroplane should land here any more
        no car with gawking tourists should stop here.
We are peaceful people and neither worship alien gods
        nor praise infamous deeds of men
Power among us is benevolent, powers from our ancestors
        power without conquest;

Once my word was venerable among Jenjewe people
Elect of spirits, I was respected and praised
Custodian of children, I devised justice, allotted land
And in calamity I offered sacrifice to the gods.
But now in gunpowder smoke I fumble at crescent
Cower under fouled air unable to lay a fire;

Violators from abroad have arrived with chisels
Borne from village to village in sedan chairs
I have watched them dismount, some monocled, cane in hand,
Scramble among hearths, gouge out old graves in the yard,
I have watched them grasp at girl's waistbeads
And barter away their sun-helmets for amulets;

For exorcism David Livingstone sent our stool to Rome
For glory Cecil Rhodes branded our cows with union jacks,
Rustled our herds off to Buckingham in cattle wagons

For a dhoti Mahatma Gandhi pawned our cowries on the Ganges
For virility Sultan Said caravanned our women to Mecca
For *lux in tenebris* Queen Victoria torched our beards
Now our favourite sons insist on hut tax and women flee south
To beauty parlours for breast punk tattoos; our men, willing
Conscripts, gnaw away the reef prospecting gems;

And you, young man
You say you are looking for fossils,
Tracking bygone patterns of migration
And death?

XXXIII
Where to Find Me

I am the one who knocks at your door at meal times
        and you do not answer,
The one who greets you when you're in intimate company
        and you do not acknowledge;

        Look for me under your feet: I'm the slug
        You trample when you stroll
        The deadwood you kick aside from picnic paths
        The weed you slash and burn in your garden.

I am the one whose call you don't hear
        as you hurry for appointments,
The one whose warning you don't heed
        as you sit in jetplanes;

        Look for me in farflung places: I'm the lice
        Burrowed in seams of your clothes
        The dirt at the centre of your back
        The itch on the spot your hands cannot reach.

At crescent moon
Look for me in fireside stories that children sing
I am the sigh in the audience,
When rain falls
Look for me in pock marks of leaves that survive autumn
I am the centre space in the rainbow,
At sunrise
Look for me in dewdrops that form at dawn

I am the vanishing point in sun's rays,

I am Fate's guest at your ignored feast,
The riff-raff who cleans your mouldering board.
I do not go away.

XXXIV
Easter at Embangweni

From all over the land they converge on
Embangweni at Easter, they come on foot
bicycles, ox carts ... curious atheists,
bored villagers who come for memories
gather with church-going peasants. In candle light
the faithful confess and ask for forgiveness.
They read the bible together in vigils and song,
weep in resonance and curse those who killed Jesus
Christ, and consummate fellowship of rededication
in choral melodies, sweat, passion, anger, fear
oozing in echoes from Embangweni church walls.
Many among us, says the minister, have been wounded
with spears sticking in our chests. Heal us, oh Lord...
Then comes a rushing of wind as people speak
in tongues - a thousand voices drone in echo.
When benediction is pronounced
the faithful disperse and move away. Others wait
to pose for photographs on the altar steps
and stroll through the sites of Easter masses,
mindful not to invert the multitude of crosses
lining the pathways. Next year,
they think, others may be here.
Not another word is said, until next year.

XXXV
Palsied Tyrant

(for Jack Mapanje)

Still the flutter of withered leaves
Along routes of armed motorcades

Still whimpers of the starving
Dispossessed

Still mute tears at midnight
for the disappeared

And the cramps, the ordeal
Of gyrating crones

Living with a palsied tyrant
that scorns his subjects.

XXXVI
They Took Suzgo Away

We all knew him
the student called Suzgo,
we admired him
for lively orations
on campus;

He drilled us about
Nkrumah and O.A.U.,
Dutschke, Guevara...
but about himself
said nothing;

SB police
started probing into
Suzgo's activities,
beliefs, ideas,
social background...

One day Suzgo was taken
away in a black jeep
blazoned with a rising sun:
"Lux in tenebris".

XXXVII
Marginals

Four brothers and a cousin
Lived together in a cardboard-
And-plastic shack
On the east edge
Of the bright city

People in lighted houses
Did not really know of their existence.
Food was scarce
So were clothes and shelter
But they had to live

When I knocked at their door
The leader opened a slat, cagily.
Dimly I saw the others stare
Playing cards, two suits draped
On rafters, a Bob Marley love song
Effusing from a corner.
They too have to live.

XXXVIII
Getting Past the Darkside
(for Orton Ching'oli Chirwa)

I
I walk, falter, listen to aches in my joints,
alone or with inmates,
I creak step by step, wade under floodlights,
edge fence heights trimmed with glass.
I trip, sometimes, peeping at the moon,
and hasten along grey walls
trying to get past the dark side.
I pace up and down, even at noon,
I shuffle my feet in circles
halt when my stomach churns.
Barefoot, like Abebe Bikila*
I run, charge round greasy pillars
and handrails that at a touch
rattle like old bones in their echoes.
Dripping wet as from a douche,
I jog, aim to dash to recover sanity.
I slip, sometimes, slamming my face into the wall,
drip on the cement floor from my mouth

II
At break of day
in solitary block
sunrays transverse my floor
through a crack in the wall,
and with a rattle I stretch my hands.
I supplicate,
reach for space in the middle,

I yearn for a touch of the divine rays.
With desperate thrust I grasp the sun
and pull it to my bosom,
but nothing holds.

Daily I see dark eclipse walls
as I pace round and round the dingy room.
Going past one wall, then another, a third
and a fourth before coming back
to the first, I circle like seasons.
Now my hair is grey, my sight is gone.

Sometimes
in the dark quiet of day
I sit cross-legged, screening
the past on grey walls.
I recall beauty of youth,
melody of nature, and free air
that roams over vales and brooks,
lavendering busy bees with scent of flower
and sunshine. Miles beyond humps
of tropical velds. Springtime
come in grass waves amid chirrup
of birds and sway of the deciduous
relaying return of seasons.
Clink! A change of gate guards I'm sure
and rise to my exercises.

---

*The Ethiopian athlete who won the Olympic marathon bare foot.

XXXIX
The Noose

The government agent read
the decree to the elders: the village
land, it said, had been sold to an estate
farmer and we were to move at once
to the hills.

We went on a last hunt
my dogs and I
we ranged the hills and beyond
but not a hare to be seen,
then we rounded the velds
and combed stream thickets.
The dogs only howled in boredom.

As we retreated homeward one dog
sniffed loudly and barked again.
I rushed in expectation and relief:
The bush, as if in stoop to first rains
buckled under the defiant poise
of village headman Chidongo.

XL
Charred Pegs
(for Vera Chirwa)

Many fail to walk out of small rooms
perfumed with smouldering cigarette studs
leftovers from midnight confessions.
Others, "stubborn", are shot in their "stubbornness",
their bodies left on lonely roads for hyenas.
And less fortunate ones face slow death of
hunger. When we toured Zomba prison
with police escort, survivors crawled back into their
cells, yet they all insisted "they keep no
prisoners here," as the gate clinked:

At his birthday anniversary
the life president twitched
when we, safe with foreign press tags,
reported the body-count from Mikuyu:
blind-folded men had been dragged
from their cells, kicking, raving themselves
hoarse. "We keep no prisoners here,"
the life president insisted:

At Kanjedza, towns people whispered,
next to the paramilitary camp,
there is a fence round lush grass and green
shrubs. Underneath the grass, they said,
there were rows and rows of red-brown
mounds - dumb witness
to those who didn't make it,
the ones who are no longer prisoners.

XLI
Austin, Frank and I

This here on my right is Austin
        witty, engaging,
And on my left, tall, islandborn
        is Frank;
We went to school together,
        intellects of our age.
Now one is missing, the other in exile;

Austin walked campus streets
Like Socrates
Engaged students in dialogue,
Tested assumed views, an advocate
Of learning, logic, and human rights.
Frank, renowned for his songs
(In his Likoma dialect)
Charmed his audiences hushed
With moonlit tales.
They went abroad to become
More refined, left me here,
A prey to fear;

The coroner said
When left idle intellect will
In fortification
Immortalize itself - Socrates,
Took of hemlock.
In this damp dark cage
I console myself with this image

Of Austin, Frank and me
Encrusted in the inner seams of
my breast.

Austin returned, I recall,
(a patriot as always)
A victim still
Of the palace guards.
Did Frank choose exile?

XLII
Freeing the Barbarians

We veered from the motorcade,
and rode up to the stone-throwing barbarians.
They, in turn, let fall their cloaks
and fled into the thickets.
They clucked like a jumble of chickens
as we shot them down

We descended and set fire to their village.
The women howled curses
at our badges shining in the bonfire.
Yelling of women is worse than men's
so we shut them up forever
and went our way.

At sundown we marched up to our camp
in proper formation
brandishing our rifles to the cheers of our men.
Let the smouldering ruins
we left behind
be a warning to all who curse us.

XLIII
Charged with Treason

(for the mother of Amnon Phiri)

We will remember her

I

To city dwellers she was thought ignorant:
She ate raw mushrooms and fried termites,
And saw the world flat and still.
She was the old grass thatch rutted by rats in heat.
To Christian zealots she was thought pagan:
She knew that things that move at night
Were not just spook owls and grunting beasts
But missioned men and women
Who knock on people's doors so late.

II

She was the mute whose enchanting song was never heard.
The old village woman had great pride in her son, Amnon:
Accused of sheltering him from baton-carrying trackers,
Charged and found guilty of harbouring a terrorist at Mzoma,
She was sentenced to be hanged, but her old age
Commuted her to crumbs of salty bread at Mikuyu prison,
Where she sat all day cross-legged,
Waking each morning to stare at the sunrise
And a world she no longer recognized from dreams.

III

Believe me, we children of Embangweni wept the day she died.
She was the brittle bundle of firewood waiting for a match,
She was the shiny set of marbles for our game at the village kraal,
She was the melodious village song that we had all learned to sing,

She was our village grandmother taken away by the Special Branch police.
And we, village children, clustered round her grave in anger.

We will remember her!

XLIV
War Birds

Glossy, black-bellied flocks of wattled
Starlings range the bushveld like nomads,
Chattering gregariously and spewing
Waterberries on riversand. Sunbirds, in
Varied plumage and rapturous in courting,
Hum to tropical blossom of honeysuckles.
A streaked woodpecker in trill-like chitter
Chisels rapid taps on a dead branch, loops
From base to top and flies to the next tree.
To us herdsboys, evening comes in stutters
Of guineafowls roosting together in large
Fig trees, lending vibrance to valley air.

Beyond a single season waves of other birds, white,
Tagging along a bald eagle, sail from winter north,
Silhouettes against the bright sun. Casting ensigns
Of chill on foliage, they rev up their wings and flap
Over the valley like locusts. Frightful! Sunbirds
Scamper to mountain tops, thirsting for revenge.
A green-glossed paradise flycatcher, flitting through
Undergrowths like an orange flame, drills fledglings
In erectile ruffs... and remember, the meek shall
inherit this earth! In ensuing scraps we, urchins
without the herd, surge out of our vantage points
with bows and arrows to sling the invaders out.

XLV
Dance of a Guerilla

Crude drum harmonics,
reverberating, exorcising,
permeate midnight air
against a compelling quietude
of nude forest moonlight;

A guerilla in fatigues
merges into the village fervour
and gyrates to rhythms and songs
praising his gun
in hastening dawn;

Fear stricken colonizers
in a hushed tropical jungle
wade in file through dew
to the glitter of their rifles
lost amid dawn glimmers of liberation.

XLVI
I Was Sent For

I was sent for,
As happens in our country. That morning,
I lighted the mine shaft for the last time
And proceeded in haste on the long journey home:
Miles by air, mile by land, Welkom to Mzimba.
I travelled through gentle land peopled with white thorns,
On a day that looked endless.
As I approached my village kraal in rainless heat
A pair of wagtails rose to a roof, whistling in flight,
Bobbing and darting; in the sadness of their whistles
I heard my mother's voice telling of "reprisals"
Mounted against our people, our charred countryside,
Our hungry children. She had written,
"The government thinks we are the enemy!"
I remembered our ancestors in rock paintings
For ever trapped in the searing granite.
I looked at the trees and thought, "A curse on informers!
For our children's sake we must fight."
I have been sent for.
It has happened before in our country.

XLVII
The Anvil

In the old village
time was measured in sledging thuds
and the roar of the goatskin bellows.
As the initiate at the anvil,
early in the morning
I would trudge over to work all day
at the anvil. My father would hammer away
at wrought iron, shaping it into hoes,
sickles, mat needles, axes and ankle-bells.
As for me, I would work the bellows sit back
filing trinkets and reaping knives,
and watch my father's hand.

One day a government lorry carried us
and all our belongings to the hill camp.
Our land had been decreed "development area",
we were told. They broke my fathers nose
and we carried him on a stretcher.
We brought out hoes, hammers, and bellows,
and we buried them, and everything else,
into the ground: there was no space for them
in the lorry. After all, I thought,
they won't be of any use where we're going,
the old man being in such a shape.
When he left us two days later, I didn't know
how to bury him, there being no hoes
with which to dig the earth.
We threw him into a shallow grave,

and hyenas laughed all night.

I left the camp later that year,
promoted to development officer
charged with collecting levy from estate squatters.
Then I was sent away south on another promotion,
and I bought a house and a Cadillac car.
I sometimes think about my people
whom I have not seen in years now
(for northerners are no longer welcome here).

XLVIII
We Shall Be At The End

We are of whirlwind, fire, rain and dust,
a spark in the eddies at the solstice, primordial,
the shadow between the super nova and the milky way
god called us by name and so we were
in the beginning, have always been and
will be in the end
for we are the end, nobody comes after us,
we are a speck of dust in the galaxy reshaped by
beams from the fiery sun that freckled our face:
we are the breed to symbolize all that might be
as we were in the beginning, have always been,
so shall we be at the end
for we are the end, nobody comes after us:
with our bare hands we built the Great Wall,
set the Stonehenge down, moulded the pyramids,
hewed the Aztecs rocks, created Tumbuktu,
crafted the Zimbabwe, brick by brick, stone by stone;
like swallows, flinging caution to the winds,
we crossed from the north pole to Antartica on bark,
painted cave rocks with marks of our existence
we invented the fire, wheel, sickle, mallet, and the loom,
fostered Buya Nehanda, Gandhi, and the Zapatistas;
grew the fig usurpers Hitler and Ceausescu ate to rise so
tall
we wretched of the earth, toilers, tillers of the land
shall rise again to claim what is ours, for we were
and shall be at the end

XLIX
Ululations to a New Moon

I rose in the dark one day, awakened
By sweet melodies clearing dawn. There was
A bustle in the village stirring the air,
A retinue of girls in a coming out ceremony
Returning from the stream pool, stomping
About, ululating to the new moon;

It is like this every time round,
Cleansed initiates glazed in ochre, ash,
And green colours huddling home in fervour
From festivals of the new season, singing,
Dancing to enjoin the cycle, jingling
The waistbeads to the phased crescent;

The air became lighter, mist rose from
The valley and I shivered in the doorway waiting
For sunrise, enthralled utterly by enchanting
Echoes that lingered on from reed flutes
Mingling with the wind and receding with sun's
Rays, prompting idle talk of fortunes to come.

L
Strolling Down the Shoreline

I had returned from the field exhausted
and after a nap I set my room alight
and decided to stroll down the shoreline.
I sauntered along pebbles in the dark
feeling shingles whip my feet, waves
roar incessantly against flashes of fireflies.
Thick clouds were emerging over the water
and I knew that soon they would blot out
the moon, making the water darker.

I listened to thuds of my feet
and thought of the void in my heart,
the loneliness at midnight. I saw you
many, many miles away, and hastened
to my room. I took pen, ink and paper
to tell you, many many miles away,
about shingles, roar of the waves,
and darkness in my heart...
But not a single word appeared on paper.

LI
Didn't We?

She first came to me in dreams only
And I was sure that when she walked abroad
I would recognize her soignée haire bathe in aloe,
And those dimples hidden by her abundant lips.
One day as I sipped from my cup
She took form, fragrant and lustrous,
Revealed like a shadow in falling flakes
Among the din and chatter of a carefree throng.
She now appears all over
Rising out of the earth, smiling behind bushes,
Jogging on hillsides and stretching everywhere
Like tropical orchids beneath morning's sun.

I began to seek her in likely places:
I wanted to scan the hills with a honeybird!
I wanted to rake the thickets with a leopard!
I wanted to range the velds with a gazelle!
I hoped the earth had not so soon
Entombed those delicate petals.

She still came to me in dreams only
And I was sure that if she walked in broad daylight
I would recognize her soignée hair bathed in aloe
And her slim wrists braceletted with amber.
One day as I sat above the honeysuckle haze
On a hill bluff, recalling sad old stories....
Behold! Didn't she take the pebbled river path
Sauntering, jeweled eyes turned dawn by the sun

And breasts pushing forward the valley wind?
Didn't she turn and say she couldn't stay?
And didn't we climb the sandy path
hand in hand, like cattle egrets, wildebeests,
The one darker and the other lighter? Didn't we?
And will she come again, wearing blossoms as before?

LII
Courting Tasiyana

I will pay her court, Tasiyana,
The shell-necked girl with sunspots
Who is beautiful as flowers in season,
Whose neck is long and skin is silk.

After the old Ngoni tradition
I will wear glossy beads in my headband
And sing like a thrush in season
In a voice full-throated with love.

If she delights in dancing
I will dance the ingoma dance
To women's chants and hand-claps,
Jabbing my spear to the rhythm of my ankle bells.

I will lull her into a trance with my footwork
And, like cattle egrets, like birds of paradise,
We will travel the luminous velds of the Vipya
Where doves reside, and spring breaks into flowers.

Like people possessed, Tasiyana and I will leap into the air
Into the mutoyi-toyi dance of the gumba-gumba
Rhythming our bodies, like mid-current reeds,
We will vibrate ourselves flat on our backs.

Who bore them, people will ask, who trained their limbs?
For we will dance with the passion of our souls.
And afterwards straggle home, lost in waves of
Endless green that sparkles into the bulbul's song.

LIII
Paying Lobola

I have told my elders at the kraal
Tasiyana is the girl I love,
But my father (thinking of lobola)
Says I cannot marry her.
"She's one of our clan" he says.
"She's your sister."

Gosh! How many heads of cattle
Add up to love?
How many pieces of gold
Buy a Tumbuka girl?
How many young men must die
Wandering frost-covered tea estates
Looking for cattle?
Or cower under the rand reef
Snuffling fatal dust, looking
For pieces of gold?
How many shall die before convention
Bends to the truth of our love?

Sometimes, on the first moon,
I hear Tasiyana's voice from an opposite
Ridge rise above mortar-and-pestle thuds
Lamenting over the loneliness
That comes with moonless nights.
In the silence of stars
I sit alone with my zither,
The crescent moon edging

Towards stringed laments of my love,
Hoping my love, like scent merging
with wind, might mingle irrevocably
With her song until an immutable union
Is born on the waves.
And my heart rises
And my voice rises
In twanged resounds
To echo our union with stars
And shimmering crescent.

LIV
Maria's Photograph

The beauty of my love is the rainbow colours
Of sun's rays in dewdrops (only more radiant)
Eliciting echoes from stars.
Her eyes sparkle like diamond's sparkles
Her neck is balanced like giraffe's,
Her poise is majestic like a palm tree unswaying.
Yet stars are endurable
Like the firmaments they are
While my love's beauty is brittle like glass
That at a snap shatters into a thousand bits;

Mr. photographer, take a picture of Maria,
Frame the image for me to keep
That captures those features I admire:
The glitter in her eyes, the crystal in her teeth
The twinkling smiles that reach to the moon,
Brown earth her skin, soignée black her hair
Glistening as she tills the rain-washed garden...
Please, take a picture of Maria
And frame it for me to keep;

But a photograph fades with time
Edges chip, frame wastes,
Sheen rubs off with constant hands
And the texture of Maria I admire
Will relapse into the brown-grey of age.
I would rather weave Maria into song
Hummed whenever this page is sung,
I would sing her features for ever.

LV
Perdita

You left without farewell, Perdita,
left your clothes behind
saying you wanted to travel light.
For months
you talked on and on about the city,
where, you said, neoned street lights
flicker throughout the night.
That is where you wanted to be, it was clear,
among long-waisted standby women
in amazing designs and chandelier earrings.
You said you yearn for those sleek
glamourous city boys with sequined
bolero jackets in patriotic red, green,
and black outmatching
discotheques flashes of blue, yellow, blue...
It's flares of fashion girls you want, you said,
a side-draped chiffon cocktail dress with
crushed bodice of gold and iridescent sequins,
a full gathered skirt with a touch of India
here and there, and lots of scarves, full-
flowing pants and sleeves with mirrors,
organza poufs on shoulder and stole.

Living with simpletons
eating dried pumpkin leaves without cumin
or coriander, or a coca-cola to neutralize
the hot chillies is not for you, you said --
You are no "bushwoman!" The jet age

has gone us by, you observed, we still live
in the ways of the bow-and-arrows.
Our jungle vapours make you puke,
so you left at dawn without farewell.
I wake up every night since you left,
grope in the dark, and stand by the door
Listening to nightingales cooing to their mates,
Gazing at stars, scanning the milky way
for signs of your return.
Morning rays bring light to my house
and I turn from the window, avoiding
your cotton dashiki with beaded lace halter neck
draped on the rafters, hanging limp.
Free at last like mountain birds in season
stories of her conquests of phased neon glamours
have sown seeds of wander in my heart
And I can no longer sleep at night.

LVI
A Letter to Anjana

Why do you have to follow me
wherever I go? When I wage along
college corridors I see your ambling
silhouette slouching criss-crossing
my path, peeping behind crevices -
why do you have to follow me so wherever I go?

When I sit in my room
in the quiet of the evening reading
news reports on African famine, Olympics...
suddenly I hear frantic raps on the door
- as if to say "open up! I know what's going on in there..." and, pushing
my papers aside, you summon me
to the ravings of your heart - why
do you have to follow me so wherever I go?

One day I went to a students' rally
and as I stood to address the crowd
I felt your presence fluffing in the throngs
nudging others to mark this point
or that in my oration - thanks, Anjana,
but why do you follow me so
wherever I go?

At the dance festival
I wanted to emmerse my soul
and dissolve myself in exorcising rhythms

of feminine incantations, but in mild-frenzy
I sensed, close behind, a tap on the shoulder
and wondered why do you follow me so
wherever I go?

Early one morning on vacation
when I passed by your village across the Rukuru
I heard amidst the stampeding mortarside
staccato and pestle thuds a sharp voice
tearing through cold dawn like a hunter's
arrow. In recognition, I swerved
wondering why we meet so
wherever I go;

Do you remember
the dazzling portrait you brought
descanting on your amorous smile,
black soignée hair, and the trinketted
ear-rings you stripped and sanctified
to ultimate union of our hearts?
You placed a gold ring on my finger,
a guardian of your love, you said,
and I was touched, entranced at the sight
of its lustre. Then, the spell over,
I cast off the enchanted ring with a warning
to you not to follow me
wherever I go;

Don't you realise
Tradition is against us
      because of our clan's enmity
Our friends are against us
      because of jealousy
Your parents are against us
      because they want you for someone else
Our enemies are against us
      because they hate us
My mother is against us
      because she doesn't want us hurt?
You follow me, you say,
Because you love me so
And I stand enthralled
Wherever you go.

LVII
Strange Ways

I

She lives in the neighbourhood
    each Sunday she passes by
my mother's house on her way to church,
    the talk of the village.
Old women gossip about her,
    they tell me she is no good
that she is loose and unwise in the ways
    of the clan.
She goes away to the city, they say,
and flirts with Indian merchants -
"Modernity has ushered her soul
    to the cosmetics of the eyebrow,
She's dyed her skin and almost burnt
    her hair."
People tell her not to overdo
    the make-up
but I am tied to her.

II
Song of a Flirt

You are but a flirt, Ndindase,
And give false hopes of marriage;
You cannot pull back the hands of time
And your back grows barky every day
Your face wrinkles like leather in moss,

> One word in your favour,
> You have the brain of a genius,
> And your poise seems ageless.

Your legs are clumsy like an armadillo's
And your arms bloated like lead pipes;
Your back thickens at the base like a bull's
And your sides are cracked and faded -
A skin become cosmetically immune.

> One word in your favour,
> You led the youths in battle,
> And proved indefatigable;

Your hair sheds and greys
Dye washes away with secretion of age
Your eyes have lost their wrinkle of conquest
Age and not polish paints your fingernails -
What youth is attracted to wilted scent?

> One word in your favour,
> Your orations to shanty dwellers
> Inspire and bewitch like succulent moans;

You are married to the struggle, you say,
But when you are crushed and wringed into hemless
Tangle of flesh, your warm linings withered and cold,
Your joints powerless in gyration
Do you think I'll make the time to praise,
Or even to chide? Not one word, my dear.

LVIII
Do You Remember?

Do you remember when we stood by the archway
At Chichiri bus stop?
Do you remember how they told me I was god
And you believed them?
I remember Chiperoni winds descending
From Mulanje Mountain, scattering red dust
All over town, covering you from head to toe
With ashen foil which you mistook for gold dust.
And market women scraped your feet until you bled,
You limped down the steps to Matenje hospital,
Do you remember? I took myself to the capital
Intending to mediate the tangled tongues,
When on smooth asphalt the car somersaulted.
Some died, but I survived, though
Collapsed into unconsciousness, my knee caps
Shattered, my ribs seared in metal shreds.
And you had thought I was a god!

LIX
The Feet of a Dancer
(for Natasha, watching her play the viola)

Some healer, perhaps, in the magic of her past
taught her to sing in unison with the seasons.
Neck outstretched, preening as a locking wagtail,
unfettered, hands flicking, she plays the harp and sings.

Then she starts dancing. I say
it is her soul, those feet, as nimble in grace
as a gazelle's in the Savannah. Her gait glazed in the dim light,
her feet rapping, she rises, widely framed beauty.

My eyes flutter and I fly back many years to Thoza:
the green brooks where I grew up, where
neighbours and game share the same spaces,
in a flash I fly twenty-some years and recall

Another dancer: glazed in the wind, turning to her vimbuza dance,
she raps into ankle-bells, pausing,
waiting for the call of my drum, poised,
walking rows of gleaming initiates – what can I do
but let linger my gaze on the luminous flush of her nipples.

I say: I have heard your voice in the fields at home,
and I call it the scented sun flowers of the veld,
the creek orchids in bloom
before they extinguish their thunder-red life.

I say: I have seen your feet cut up the plateaux
and I call them rivulets and groves of the veld,
water that colours and livens the land, flowing
from thunder, which is the sound your dance makes.

LX
Search for a Bride

Lubani lavender will give her away,
Or else her melodious voice.
I will move in ivory light at dawn
Comb ridge after ridge of the green landscape,
For I am the shell-necklace lover of the hills,
Intent on finding Tasiyana for a bride.
Only the speckled pigeon's cooing
Can explain to me now, note by note,
Why I should stop the search for my bride.
I will know her, I am certain,
But the mark of her bracelet,
The sunspots on her shell necklace.
I will woo her with the nimble feet of an ingoma dancer,
I will unlace her sunbrown mountain sandals, and
Untie her loin cloth of black, red and green,
Bright like flames on the lake,
And I will engulf her with the fire of my loins.
But should any mortal come between her and me
I will turn to the sun and blind her with my blood.

www.ingramcontent.com/pod-product-compliance
Lightning Source LLC
Chambersburg PA
CBHW070334230426
43663CB00011B/2303